LITT

CA

A parent's guide to the
little star of the family

JOHN ASTROP

with illustrations by the author

ELEMENT

Shaftesbury, Dorset ● Rockport, Massachusetts
Brisbane, Queensland

Published in Great Britain in 1994 by
Element Books Ltd.
Longmead, Shaftesbury, Dorset

Published in the USA in 1994 by
Element, Inc.
42 Broadway, Rockport, MA 01966

Published in Australia in 1994 by
Element Books Ltd.
for Jacaranda Wiley Ltd.
33 Park Road, Milton, Brisbane, 4064

Printed and bound in Great Britain by
BPC Paulton Books Ltd.

British Library Cataloguing in Publication
data available

Library of Congress Cataloguing in publication
data available

ISBN 1-85230-540-1

CONTENTS

THE TWELVE SIGNS

Everyone knows a little about the twelve sun signs. It's the easiest way to approach real astrology without going to the trouble of casting up a chart for the exact time of birth. You won't learn everything about a person with the sun sign but you'll know a lot more than if you just use observation and guesswork. The sun is in roughly the same sign and degree of the zodiac at the same time every year. It's a nice astronomical event that doesn't need calculating. So if you're born between

May 22 and June 21 you'll be pretty sure you're a Gemini; between June 22 and July 23 then you're a Cancer and so on. Many people say how can you divide the human race into twelve sections and are there only twelve different types. Well for a start most people make assessments and judgements on their fellow humans with far smaller groups than that. Rich and poor, educated and non-educated, town girl, country boy, etc. Even with these very simple pigeon holes we can combine to make 'Rich educated town boy' and 'poor non-educated country girl'. We try to get as much information as we can about the others that we make relationships with through life. Astrology as a way of describing and understanding others is unsurpassed. Take the traditional meaning of the twelve signs:

Aries - is self-assertive, brave, energetic and pioneering.

Taurus - is careful, possessive, values material things, is able to build and make things grow.

Gemini - is bright-minded, curious, communicative and versatile.

Cancer - is sensitive, family orientated, protective and caring.

Leo - is creative, dramatic, a leader, showy and generous.

Virgo - is organised, critical, perfectionist and practical.

Libra - is balanced, diplomatic, harmonious, sociable, and likes beautiful things.

Scorpio - is strong-willed, magnetic, powerful, extreme, determined and recuperative.

Sagittarius - is adventurous, philosophical, far-thinking, blunt, truth-seeking.

Capricorn - is cautious, responsible, patient, persistent and ambitious.

Aquarius - is rebellious, unorthodox, humanitarian, idealistic, a fighter of good causes.

Pisces - is sensitive, imaginative, caring, visionary and sacrificing.

If you can find anyone in your circle of friends and acquaintances who isn't described pretty neatly by one of the above it would be surprising. Put the twelve signs into different lives and occupations and you see how it works. A Taurean priest would be more likely to devote his life to looking after the physical and material needs of his church members, feeding the poor, setting up charities. A Virgoan bank robber would plan meticulously and never commit spontaneous crimes. A Leo teacher would make learning an entertainment and a pleasure for her pupils.

So with parents and children. A Capricorn child handles the business of growing up and learning in a very different way to a Libran child. A Scorpio parent manages the family quite differently to an Aquarian. The old boast, 'I'm very fair, I treat all my children the same', may not be the best way to help your little ones at all. Our individual drive is the key to making a success of life. The time when we need the most acceptance of the way we are is in childhood. As a parent it's good to know the ways in which our little ones are like us but we must never forget the ways in which they are different.

LITTLE CANCER

For the whole gamut of emotions this is the child who'll come up with the widest range in the shortest possible time. Tears and chuckles, gloom and gurgles of delight, loving hugs that would crush the life out of you and sulks that freeze all attempts at consolation. Everything this little fellah experiences is going into a memory bank that will last all his lifetime and don't you forget it. The most powerful influences in the lives of Cancerians happen in the early years around the family. They never forget those years and how well they manage the rest of their lives depends a great deal on how well they came through them. Sounds daunting, doesn't it? Not on your sweet life, for once you realise that they are probably the most sensitive and caring children in the zodiac you can prepare yourself for the most perfect child any parent could wish for. The Cancer child doesn't rush into unknown territory risking bruised head and broken bones. You won't lose them in the Supermarket, in fact you'll have a job letting go of their

hot little hands. They won't ever speak to strangers (often not even to new friends that you might wish them to meet). All in all, the fact that they cry a little more (in fact, to be honest they cry quite a lot!) when they're unhappy is a small price to pay

 for the lack of worry you'll have about where they are and what they're doing when you can't see them. They make perfect children because they are in training to become perfect parents. Few other children will get so much pleasure out of 'helping' Mom or Dad. It will not take long to realise that what may seem just 'crybabyness' is deep sensitivity to the moods and feelings of others. Little Crabs protect themselves but they also protect you and everyone else that they hold dear. Their weakness is their greatest strength, 'caring', and probably you will never really understand the Cancerian strength until they become your 'shoulder to cry on' in

later life. For all the sensitivity, like the crab, the softness is all inside. The outer shell of a Cancerian allows them to be as tough as old nails in the harsh world of commerce. Many become really successful business people and most of them will have their own businesses. The fact that they run them just like families is quite noticeable in their caring attitude to staff and conditions. Their offices are probably the most homey and comfortable you can find, more often antique than high tech. So little Cancer with all this potential, imagination and artistic ability will be a challenge for you to stimulate and develop. The ability to empathise and feel not only other's feelings but visualise imaginary events as if they were real, enables many little Cancerians to become good actors, authors and artists. Listen, when your little Crab is talking and playing with her imaginary friend who sits on the end of her bed every morning, and you'll recognise the talent and want to do all you can to develop it.

THE BABY

Changeable like the moon that rules his sign, the baby Cancerian will move from mood to mood each time you pick him up and you'll pick him up a lot. There's a vulnerability in these little bundles of feeling that brings out the maternal instinct, even in the most 'matter of fact' old Dad, and gets them just the right amount of cuddles on which they

thrive. Quick to remember and enjoy what he liked the last time, all new experiences will be accompanied with well expressed pleasure or spat out or brushed away with tears of disappointment. In no uncertain terms they like what they like and hate what they don't. Small moon children start talking with their expressive faces long before they could possibly mouth the first words. Not just the smiling, crying or sleeping of most children but a whole gamut of expressions that change in a flash from a sarcastic smirk to a disapproving frown. Occasionally you'll notice the big blue eyes of your little Cancer have misted over and a gentle smile on the face of your babe that makes her seem to be a thousand miles away. She's practising the Cancerian ability to tune in and understand deep inside, every sound, every colour, and every movement that surrounds her small world.

THE FIRST THREE YEARS

Your tiny Cancer will not be in a hurry to move on to each new stage of development. Everything is taken in on a totally feeling level and there is great caution in opening themselves to new experiences until the old ones are fully assimilated. In the first couple of years you will be delighted to see what a great talent the little Crab has for mimicry. It will not be long before their little collection of cuddly toys, cars and trucks become a 'family' and even before they have more than a few words you'll catch them doing a passable imitation of you, tending to their little one's needs. You will find their sensitivity tunes into your moods and responds accordingly; this means that they laugh more and cry more than most children even just bursting into tears because you look a little grumpy or off colour. Although emotionally you'll become all too aware of little Cancer's vulnerability, great care should be taken not to over protect them from the harsh world outside or you will later find problems with getting them to nursery school.

Little crabs have tough shells, and they need them with all that soft sensitive stuff inside. You'll have to help them in the discovery of this vital defence and get them used to the crab's second line of protection, the sidestep. Their caring  nature makes them worry about everything and you'll have to teach them that there are just too many things to carry on such small shoulders. Happiest times at this stage will be when all the family gather together and these occasions will be remembered throughout their sentimental lives and become a tradition to be passed on to their own families.

THE KINDERGARTEN

Even if you've put in a great deal of ground work easing your little Cancer into the realities of the outside world, you may still find Junior clinging to your legs when this drastic change in routine occurs. Insisting and getting cross will not achieve anything so it's back to the reassuring cuddles and promises of cosy get togethers afterwards that are more likely to work. It may take a time but in the  end little Cancer will see the nursery school as a family extension and start mothering her very best friends. It's here that the real qualities of the caring Cancerian will begin to show. This small nurse, boy or girl, will console little friends whether their troubles are a bruised elbow or a snatched toy.

Surprisingly enough, she will even reassure other little Cancerians that their Mummy will be along later to pick them up. In no time at all your little shrinking violet will have gained confidence, know where everything is, remember what they all do at what time and proceed to gently organise and 'look after' the newer members of the playgroup.

SCHOOL AND ONWARDS

Joining yet another 'family' may initially produce a few teething problems but past experience will usually help little Cancer deal with this new adventure. This period will be a delight to you, for this is where the Cancerian sensitivity and versatile imaginative talents will start to bear fruit. The day's events will be recounted and elaborated, little Cancer soon developing a real ability for embellishing the duller stories and giving them a touch more romance. The

sharing of the school gossip (amusingly enhanced) will be a delight and an entertainment that you will look forward to daily. This is also a good way for Junior to link you closely with the life he spends away from home. School work, with the advantage of a Cancer's perfect memory, will be comfortable but as these little ones remember most easily by feelings, they will make little effort to achieve any distinction in a subject that doesn't move them. History, stories and real life accounts have the greatest appeal for Cancerians with their ability to translate them into vivid imaginary pictures, enabling the images to remain with them throughout life.

THE THREE DIFFERENT TYPES OF CANCERIAN

THE DECANATES

Astrology traditionally divides each of the signs into three equal parts of ten degrees called the decanates. These give a slightly different quality to the sign depending on whether the child is born in the first, second or third ten days of the thirty-day period when one is in a sign. Each third is ruled by one of the three signs in the same element. Cancer is a Water sign and the three Water signs are Cancer, Scorpio and Pisces. The nature of Water signs is basically feeling and emotional so the following three types each has a different way of expressing these qualities.

First Decanate - June 22 to July 1

This is the part of Cancer that is most typical of the sign qualities. The Sensitive Traditionalist. Ruled by the fluctuating moon the moodiness is probably more pronounced than the other two decanates. Their sense of the value of things and feelings from the past make them compulsive collectors of valuable antiques and historical anecdotes, but also pieces of everyday trivia that others would deem junk. The latter accumulations, however, to a Cancerian represent the keys that open doors to reliving floods of vividly remembered experiences. Even your tiniest Crab will have hijacked one of your shoeboxes for an early start to just such a lifetime collection. One of these must have invented the tradition of 'something old, something blue' etc. at marriages. In later life many of these Cancerians achieve great success in fields where a sensitive tuning in to the needs and reactions of others can give them a head start in popularity.

You'll find them often in the public eye, from Princess Diana's entrancing ability to capture the hearts of millions to Mel Brooks tickling of the world's funny bone.

Second Decanate - July 2 to July 12

This is the Persuasive Traditionalist. Ruled by the powerful transforming planet Pluto and linked with the strong sign of Scorpio these are the toughest of the Cancers. If your little Cancer is born in this decanate he'll probably cry just as much when he falls, but recoup faster and tougher for the experience. You'll be surprised how soon this small Crab starts getting interested in the deep questions of death, birth, and sex and you'll have to come up with some pretty profound answers for what you say now will be always remembered. Untypically these little sensitives will take on far greater challenges than their fellow crustaceans. More prepared to battle for what they want in life and needing to be supported in what they do, there seems to be a natural magnetism in these fascinating characters that claims devoted followers. Sylvester Stallone plays the 'toughie' supreme that influences a generation, but still loves his Mom, Marc Chagall was bold enough to change a lot of people's view on art, but his subject matter was wrapped up in memories of his childhood past in Russia.

Third Decanate - July 13 to July 23

The Imaginative Traditionalist. Those born in this decanate are ruled by the planet Neptune and linked to the highly imaginative sign of Pisces. This little Cancer will invent the tallest of tall stories and have you believing them because you want to. Their reactions to others are almost psychic, tapping into their thoughts like a professional mind reader. They differ from the other two decanates in that they are attracted to far away places and spend a great deal of their lives travelling or at least with a love of distant lands and other cultures. Ernest Hemingway travelled and wrote imaginative and emotional stories on safari in Africa and during the Civil War in Spain. Julius Caesar liked far distant lands so much, he made them family.

OTHER LITTLE CANCERIANS

Mums and Dads like you delighted in bringing up the following extra sensitive little bundles. Yours will probably turn out to be even more famous!

First Decanate Cancer
John Dillinger, Empress Josephine, Franz Kafka, Jack Dempsey, George Orwell, Jean Anouilh, Charles Laughton, Meryl Streep, George Sax, Hellen Keller, Carly Simon, Henry VIII, Cyndi Lauper, Dan Ackroyd, Princess Diana, Mel Brooks.

Second Decanate Cancer

Sylvester Stallone, Herman Hesse, Jean Cocteau, Marcel Proust, Tom Hanks, Modigliani, Louis Armstrong, Marc Chagall, Leggs Diamond, Arnold Schwarzenegger, George Sand, Gustav Mahler, Beatrix Potter, Oscar Hammerstein, Neil Simon, Nancy Reagan, P.T. Barnum, Arthur Ashe, Henry Moore, Shelley Duvall, Tom Cruise.

Third Decanate Cancer

Julius Caesar, Donald Sutherland, Edgar Degas, Ernest Hemingway, Errol Garner, Earl Stanley Gardner, James Cagney, W.M. Thackeray, Ingmar Bergman, Rembrandt, Ginger Rogers, Woody Guthrie, Linda Ronstadt, Phyllis Diller, John Glenn, Carlos Santana, Diana Rigg, Robin Williams, William Defoe.

AND NOW THE PARENTS

THE ARIES PARENT

The good news!

The Aries parent is strong, self-willed, affection-ate and quick to act. Cancer always responds to the mood of the moment. This parent will encourage the child confidently to express what it feels, when it feels it. Cancer's radar tunes in to other people's highs and lows and shares them. With the Aries parent the wavelength is enthusiasm, and the po-tential positive. Powerful as they are, Aries adults rarely crush others, for their belief in the right of the individual is supreme. Junior will be supported

when necessary, but not hampered or overprotected when wanting to 'go it alone'. An ideal relationship to bring out this child's leadership potential. Little Cancerians are not, however, born to be battlers and warriors like you, the Aries parent. Rushing into new experiences is not an activity that you will persuade your little Crab to share. Life for these little traditionalists is based on what happened before. If a previous experience was good they'll try it again and be distraught if it doesn't turn out to be exactly the same. For new experiences there's no previous comforting example so they don't like 'em. Mostly you'll have to hold little Cancer's hand, physically or mentally to get him to move on to anything new. All experience for small Crabs is emotionally based and your strength will need to be subtly supportive but never obtrusive in order for the strong feelings of this child to gain in confidence and self-assurance.

...and now the bad news!

Negatively your Aries' overdrive can rush and panic Cancer into unprepared-for situations with resulting emotional disaster. Aries in their constant enthusiasm for the sheer adventure of life can remain blissfully unaware that not everybody learns to swim by jumping in the deep end, and will wonder why such an excellent child should suddenly turn into a nervous, apprehensive, and crabby crybaby. Insecure Cancerians can become the most clinging children in the zodiac and heaven help the freedom loving parent. Develop good timing and read little Cancer's signals which are always well displayed. You're both loving and affectionate and this is your key to the relationship. Plenty of cuddles and you'll be blessed with more laughter than tears. (But there'll always be a great deal of both!)

THE TAURUS PARENT

The good news!

You are steady as a rock, like material comfort and good order and let everyone know where they stand with you. The Cancerian child needs, above all, a secure protective home environment and that will certainly be well met in your almost perfect relationship. The Taurean appreciates the Cancerian child's ability to record every experience and file it away for instant recall, making learning easy. Although often moody and clinging, this is not a sign of weakness but of great sensitivity and responsiveness to people and situations. Far from being 'shrinking violets' Cancerians have leadership qualities of the good-humoured, gentle kind, given the security that comes naturally from the Taurean parent. Little Cancer builds confidence on past experience and resists moving headlong into new and unknown territory. Your Taurean pace is just about right and never pushy, for you know the value of feeling completely happy with each stage in Junior's progress before moving on to the next. Needing more than most children in terms

of emotional closeness can make the little Crabs more clinging in the early years but the Taurean Mom or Dad will not be in a hurry to lose their warm, loving baby. Quite homeloving yourself (the Bull will invest wisely a great deal of time and money on making the family home the best showplace in the neighbourhood), a great deal of shared activity will go on in the comfort of the great indoors. Cancerians are usually very creative and some kind of comfortable workshop that you can both share would be beneficial to this close relationship.

...and now the bad news!

Conflicts can occur when Taurus's fixed and well-proven ideas come up against Cancer's inexplicable 'feelings'. With common sense and obstinacy (a good Taurean combination), the Bull may be too quick to scoff at intuitive hunches. You have to be prepared for almost psychic reactions to some people and things and no amount of persuasion will change the little Cancer's feelings. It's wise to observe how many times this little crystal ball's prediction turns out to be right about someone or something you thought was a good'un through and through. Even if they're wrong however never make this a basis for a stand-up battle. Crabs, though not the most aggressive of the signs, are masters of the art of self-defence. The outer shell becomes thicker and the soft, sensitive centre that makes for such a loving and caring child will be quite firmly withdrawn.

♊

THE GEMINI PARENT

The good news!

You are versatile and intelligent, with wide interests and an ever-changing personality. Your security in the world is built on knowledge and as much information as you can pack into your busy mind. Your Cancerian child learns through feeling and personal experience rather than the accumulation of intellectual knowledge. The child's sensitivity, awareness and imagination will respond well to this parental encyclopaedia of activity and information. Gemini's interest in every thing the young Cancerian sees, feels and does, will keep the child's strong need for close relationships well satisfied. The Gemini parent's own desire for constant stimulation will expand Junior's self-expressive nature. Because, however, the little Crab is more concerned with understanding her complex feelings than just accumulating facts, the Gemini pace will often be too far ahead of this emotional child. Cancerians need time to adjust to new situations

and new ideas, they like to live with them for a long time until they're sure how they feel about them. Although yours is not the most demonstrative of signs, you will find real pleasure in little Cancer's need for plenty of hugs and cuddles. Gemini and Cancer are the moodiest signs in the zodiac, yours more a switch off when you get bored with anything, Junior's totally based on sensitive reactions to the others around. These little barometers pick up the emotional hots and colds in family life, never missing the slightest touch of tension between Mom and Dad.

...and now the bad news!

The area where clashes can occur may be found in Cancer's need to structure ideas based on past experience and Gemini's facility for dropping yesterday's truths in the light of today's discoveries. With one of you looking back and the other looking forward, a great deal of work will have to be done to make real connections when problem situations arise. Ideas are best opened up slowly and expanded rather than shattered and replaced, otherwise Cancer will be totally confused. Everything with little Cancer has to flow and have the right feeling, mental jumps and sudden revelations are not on the agenda. Little Cancers hang on to Santa Claus and the Easter Bunny longer than most. This doesn't mean they are backward in any way. The role of the Cancer throughout life is a nurturing and caring one, so remember that developing a feeling heart is not quite so fast as sharpening a wit.

THE CANCER PARENT

The good news!

Blessed with the longest memories in the zodiac, you Cancer parents have no difficulty in recalling vividly the emotions and impressions of your own childhood. Well-behaved, sensitive little Cancer will find the dream parent in this caring 'home bird' adult. The need to love and cherish is so strong in both that you may find yourselves later swapping roles. 'I'll be mummy and you be me' is a favourite Cancer game. Little Crabs learn steadily, though more through feelings and experience than textbook information. They laugh and cry easily with close friends but are cautiously shy in making new ones until they feel really secure. As you are much the same you'll never throw young Cancer into the deep end with difficult emotional situations and sudden new experiences without a great deal of preparation and rehearsal. Even if your creativity became a little crushed on your journey through the painful trip to adulthood don't forget that Cancerians are usually loaded with potential artistic ability. This impressionable youngster may hide a wealth of sensitivity and imagination if not given sufficient encouragement to express these creatively. Warm

appreciation of early efforts build good self-confidence that may eventually develop and become an important part of your little one's future life. You're a great worrier, and the talent for mentally predicting all kinds of potential disasters are of course part of your natural protective instinct. Little Cancer is made of the same stuff and will sense all your worries as soon as you have them, so try not to pass on too many problems for those tiny shoulders at too early a stage or you'll both be scared to go out of the front door!

...and now the bad news!

It would be hard to visualise a quarrel at all in this all-feeling, all-caring relationship. As mentioned above, overprotection, that's the snag. If the Cancer home becomes too much of a cosy, warm cocoon, Junior may never be brave enough to leave. Although you're happiest occupying yourself in your well made and comfortable home you'll eventually have to introduce the little Crab to the big, tough world outside. Soft as his sensitive nature seems to make him his tough outer shell can take it. Like the creature itself, you and your little one can slip sideways when the going gets tough and as a last resort pop back into that crusty exterior.

THE LEO PARENT

The good news!

You are generous, amiable, big-thinking and take a great pride in the family. The Cancer child's every achievement will be noticed, appreciated and applauded with warm pleasure. Leo's love of showmanship and creative self-expression will prove good encouragement for little Cancer's sensitivity to be expressed in positive ways. For you understand the importance of creative activity in giving confidence to this potentially talented child. Cancerians learn by experiencing the feelings and actions of others, trying things out with their superb talent for mimicry. This will be a source of delight for the Leo parent who will hope for a superstar but generously settle for a good companion if the bright lights aren't achieved. You thrive on appreciation and with this member of your family you'll get constant reassurance from the warm, demonstrative nature of the little Crab. Plenty of

hugs and kisses and of course the tears, tantrums and laughter too. You'll enjoy the whole gamut of emotions from this all-feeling and amusing little Cancerian. Never as bold as you, your little one will admire and learn from your great self-confidence and will achieve great confidence herself as long as you don't press too hard and too fast. More likely to respond to any learning project in cosy twosomes rather than group activities, you will find that Cancerians learn more easily at home than they do at school. If Mom and Dad give their support at homework time, Junior progresses by leaps and bounds.

...and now the bad news!

Negatively, big-acting Leos can be crushingly over-dramatic, always centre stage, leaving their little Cancers with minor walking-on parts, swamped and hiding nervously in the wings. You'll be appreciated if you let the understudy take the leading role sometimes. There is another side to this coin, however, and not all Leos are the fulfilled and confident beings we expect. Often frustrated Leos, who didn't quite 'make it' themselves, try to live out their own dreams through their young prodigies. This can work with other signs but rarely with a small Cancerian. Little Crabs with this treatment can spend a lifetime in their shells.

THE VIRGO PARENT

The good news!

Like all Virgos you'll run an efficient, clean, practical home and tend to the needs of others with great care and modesty. The sensitive Cancer child will be supported conscientiously at every stage of development. With a Virgo parent nothing is too much trouble. The child will be read to, washed, fed an intelligent diet, played with, entertained and educated, all with a quiet efficiency that typifies the Virgo. In this atmosphere little Cancer will develop self-assurance and a good knowledge of how to deal with the material world. Cancerians, highly imaginative, can be almost as great dreamers as Pisceans, using their fantasy world as a substitute for real and positive action. The good old Virgo trait of practicality will not, in the best possible way, let a lazy little Crab get away with this. Starting with the simplest projects little Cancer will be taught how to make ideas a reality, putting into action Junior's creative dreams and developing his talents. The little Crab learns by mimicry and at

the earliest stage will follow Mom around playing 'keeping house' and 'helping'. There will be times when Virgo's earthy practicality will find it hard to understand the Cancerian 'moods'. Sometimes almost hypersensitive to the feelings of others around her, your small light-hearted co-worker will inexplicably change to a mood of doom and gloom. Probably just remembering something sad she saw on TV but usually a loving hug will put all things right.

...and now for the bad news!

There are snags that even Virgo's good critical faculties don't always notice. In fact all that good common sense may overlook the highly imaginative, creative side of little Cancer. Little Cancers, governed so much by feeling, like to respond to things when they seem 'right'. In a regime where routine has taken over (and sometimes this works so well for Virgos that they forget lesser mortals can't take it), there is no room for the unusual and unexpected pleasure of doing things when one feels like it rather than when it's the correct time. Junior emotionally denied and a slave to routine can become a 'crabby' little character, clamping up and making communication difficult. It's not always a crime to break the rules – that's how we find our own originality and uniqueness.

♎

THE LIBRA PARENT

The good news!

Librans create beautiful homes, have an easy charming manner that rarely gets ruffled, and love good company. Cancers are delightful company. This is a relationship of beauty, love, sensitivity and close friendly conversation. Both respond well to others and young Cancer's self-expression can grow in the confidence that nothing disharmonious will disrupt this household. Not if Libra has anything to do with it. Libra can always see the other side and Cancer can always feel for the other person. What a combination for peace and good-will. Libra's love of the social life and entertaining will get the little Cancer used to being with more than a few close family members, a constant stream of visitors to the home will help to develop self-confidence in strange company. The Libran is usually a good conversationalist and the well-laid-down habit of cosy chats in the early years will develop later into easy discussions of all matters, carrying this relationship through the difficult teenage years with ease. Little Cancer will always be encouraged to express feelings verbally instead of just leaving

things to tears and tantrums. It may be well to remember though that when all else fails to console, hugs and cuddles will mean more to this sensitive little being than all the sweet talk in the world. These highly emotional and protective small Crabs will grow up to be loving, caring parents themselves and will need to try out their abilities on stray cats, a puppy, a pet earwig, but most of all on you. The more they can help Mommy and Daddy the more this little carer will thrive.

...and now the bad news!

Works a treat on one level but like any other relationship it has occasional snags if not confrontations. Libra's desire to please both sides on an issue at the same time can lead to frustrated indecision and often acute embarrassment for Junior. Little Cancer likes to know where he is in any family situation and if Mom or Dad don't seem to be able to make up their minds, that can lose, for this child, a great deal in emotional security. Cancerians do not have the ability to see all sides of any question. If they like somebody or something, great! – if they don't, no amount of rational or harmonious argument on the part of the diplomatic parent will alter the little Crab's view.

THE SCORPIO PARENT

The good news!

This is a powerful, loving relationship for you both. Highly protective, the Scorpio parent has a strong self-will, deep feelings, and builds a home that is invulnerable. Cancer needs a secure emotional and physical environment in which to grow and finds it in this relationship. Scorpios sense potential in people, situations and things and are compelled to transform raw material into positive achievement. This quality in its best form is subtle, selfless and loving and young Cancer will grow in confidence and self-reliance, enthusiastically supported in any activity or talent needing to be expressed. Although powerful in the defence of loved ones, Scorpio knows that developing the child's own inner strength is better protection against the knocks of life than stepping in to interfere at every opportunity. Little Cancer, however,

is not made of the same stuff as you and will never aspire to the almost magnetic power that you can exert over others. Your little one's strength is in learning how to tend and care for the people and things he loves and being well able to use the tough outer shell to see him through the difficult times. Confident with his feelings and encouraged to develop the good business sense and caring qualities that are typical of the well adjusted Cancerian, Junior will be a credit to the family and the sensitivity of his strong parent.

...and now the bad news!

Scorpios use their power in all kinds of ways throughout their life. When it's the power of love no one can be more devoted. Negatively, however, Scorpio can be manipulative and domineering almost without thinking, pushing little Cancer, this much more gentle being, further than is comfortable and producing a fear of failure out of all proportion to the facts. Cancers care deeply and Scorpio's disappointment can produce a lifetime of guilt. Cancerians' aims are always modest but their achievements can be great if they are emotionally stable. Remember that, seeing all life as a great challenge, your aims are way above the wildest dreams of most people, but especially little Cancer. This can be one of the closest relationships in the zodiac if you allow her to pick the role in life she hopes to attain and support her unobtrusively but devotedly.

THE SAGITTARIUS PARENT

The good news!

You are optimistic and freedom-loving with a broad understanding of life and people. Discipline is liable to be lax but that's because the Sagittarian parent will seem more like a jovial friend. Not the most adventurous of characters, little Cancer will rarely take advantage of this parent's soft approach to routine. In fact, in the right kind of environment (and that means an emotionally stable one), small Crabs tend to be helpful rather than difficult children. This any Sagittarian will love, not taking kindly to restrictions on their precious freedom. Little Cancerian's horizons will be expanded by this free-ranging parent. Travelling with mum or dad Sagittarius will open up new vistas that will not be found within the family circle, and prepare young Cancerians for the big world outside. The Sagittarian will show by example that the honest expression of what one thinks and feels is not only permissible but essential for true individual development. There will be little time for the usual 'crabby' moodiness of this child to show itself for the relationship will contain too much fun and adventure not to keep little Cancer's emotions working to the full on the positive side. Sagittarians

spend their lives educating themselves, always hungry for knowledge, and loving to learn about far away places and peoples. Little Cancer's ability to hold information, rarely forgetting anything that she has learned, will be admired, but Cancers are home loving and out of choice the far away places will be more appreciated as stories than as a practical reality.

...and now the bad news!

This all sounds so easy-going and is... unless of course the worst happens. The clashpoint in this relationship is obviously the Sagittarian desire to be unshackled and free and the Cancerian's deep emotional need to hold on. In this situation the Archer can use frank honesty and blunt hurtful home truths, and the Crab as usual is back in the shell, but not without getting that big claw firmly on the ankle of the parent, in the form of perpetual guilt. The best way to gain your own and Junior's independence is to share it. It takes an early start to get little Cancer used to the 'on the move' life of a galloping Sagittarian but it can be done. Once the little Crab has got used to what you do and where you go, and that you always come back, you'll be able to leave her behind waiting for the news of your adventures when you return. They really are home birds and only a few trips will be necessary to establish the confidence.

THE CAPRICORN PARENT

The good news!

You have an unassuming authority, love of order, and respect for the tradition of the family, building the secure home background that little Cancer needs. For Capricorn, relationships work best when there is a clearly defined but reasonable set of guidelines to keep to. The ever-changing and sometimes confusing 'feelings' of the small Cancerian soon gain confidence of expression within this secure, firm but fair arrangement. No shocks of sudden revelation will be allowed to disrupt the Capricornian home but Junior will be assisted with great care and unlimited patience in the art of never putting a foot wrong. In this safe environment, this naturally fearful child will feel no threats and be able to channel the full Cancerian imaginative talents into concrete achievement. Capricornians are as appreciative of others' abili-

ties as they are ambitious with their own. The difference in aims may have to be understood though. For the Goat, ambitions will more often than not be concerned with realistic and materialistic achievements, whereas little Cancer's growth may lie in the development of the dreamy intuitive creativity that typifies this

water sign. Good humour will be a great key to bring these two different qualities together. Although sometimes a little serious and 'cold' in their approach to everyday life, Capricorn 'silly goats' have a zany sense of the ridiculous and Cancerians are hilarious mimics when encouraged. Frequent expression of these talents should warm the relationship considerably.

...and now the bad news!

Negatively, the socially conscious Capricorn can be continuously worrying about what others think, to such a degree that their little Cancer will clam up against the rain of do's and don'ts. If you don't want your tiny Crab to develop a thicker shell and use all that soft-centre imagination in predicting the next disaster (a favourite timewasting Cancer talent) then inject the rules with a little elastic and stretch 'em. The saving grace for this possible clash is that as Capricornians get older they seem to get younger in spirit and begin to let their hair down. By the time Junior reaches the difficult teenage years the two of you can be the best of pals.

THE AQUARIUS PARENT

The good news!

You are sociable, unusual, forward-looking, detached and tolerant. Highly imaginative young Cancerians need a strong emotional rapport to bring out their exceptional caring, artistic and creative abilities. Aquarius will rarely be the dogmatic, heavy parent, but rather the helpful friend. The ability to take an unprejudiced view of any situation can be invaluable in reassuring little Cancer's biased, self-protective fears. There will be few set rules in this relationship, each situation being resolved when it arises with an open mind and little fuss. Although Cancer's desire to give and receive demonstrative affection may not be totally satisfied by the sometimes detached manner of the Aquarian parent, the child will never feel neglected. Aquarians give a great deal of time and thought to the things which fascinate their nimble minds. Your genuine interest and insatiable curiosity in the development of this sensitive child will provide a closeness that should combine with an opening up

of the normally inward looking Cancer. Your role in life, directed more towards broad thinking and a love of mankind, caring deeply about big injustices, may sometimes find stifling little Cancer's need for close one-to-one emotional bonds. Your clever logic will often be dumbfounded by your little Crab's inexplicable 'moods' and 'feelings'. Alien as they are to you, nothing really throws the odd-ball Aquarian off balance and you may even get to like the friendly close cuddles that you discover solve most of little Cancer's problems.

...and now the bad news!

The biggest factor causing rifts in this relationship is the contrast between Aquarius's future-orientated outlook and Cancer's need to live on past experience. A strange twist of parent/child behaviour. The Water Carrier will open the doors to new, unusual, and sometimes bewildering experience leaving little Cancer with a host of past experience which now seems irrelevant. Utopian Aquarians may need to take Cancer's hand a bit more convincingly into the 'Brave New World'. Face up to the fact that 'get together' things that you do will have to be repeated as your little one learns by experiencing and reliving each experience, so 'Play it again Sam'.

♓

THE PISCES PARENT

The good news!

Piscean parents are artistic, creative, highly emotional and highly imaginative. Snap! So are Cancerians. The difference is that Junior may just have the edge when it comes to down-to-earth things. This won't hurt a bit in this loving, warm, and always close relationship. The Piscean spontaneous sense of whimsy and fantasy will encourage young Cancer to experience the full range of feelings, yet never overpower Junior's own contribution to the fun, laughter and tears. The eternal child in

Pisces is totally at one with little Cancer, intuitively sensing and removing fears, or recognising and supporting signs of independence. The rose-tinted spectacles can get a little cloudy if Pisces sets Junior up on too high a pedestal. The tough Crab shell can take a few hard knocks but won't enjoy falling from a great height. Cancers hate to let their loved ones down and yet are a little more modest than Piscean dreams sometimes allow. Whether this becomes an occupation later or just something that

adds a great deal of pleasure to the quality of life, little Cancer will undoubtedly have some artistic talent that is worth encouraging. Creatively the home of a Piscean can be a perfect greenhouse for bringing into full flower little Cancer's artistic development. Pisceans always spoil their children and this child will be inundated with so much inspirational and stimulating material to work with that there should be some outstanding results.

...and now the bad news!

Almost the only problem with this near perfect cosy twosome is the very thing they have in common. Both emotionally sensitive, their 'moods' and emotional outbursts can become self-indulgent to such an extent that it passes the bounds of what would be considered OK in the outside world. Little Cancer is much more of a conventional traditionalist than you and will not be secure with having to switch to different behaviour in different circumstances. The other problem is when the moods don't coincide, when each is too aware of the other's feelings; emotions can swing back and forth at such a rate as to exasperate other members of the family. The negative Piscean reaction when all gets too much is to disappear, any form of escape being acceptable, leaving little Cancer over-stimulated and insecure. Best to keep cool and keep cosy.

ON THE CUSP

Many people whose children are born on the day the sun changes signs are not sure whether they come under one sign or another. Some say one is supposed to be a little bit of each but this is rarely true. Adjoining signs are very different to each other so checking up can make everything clear. The opposite table gives the exact Greenwich Mean Time (GMT) when the sun moves into Cancer and when it leaves. Subtract or add the hours indicated below for your nearest big city.

AMSTERDAM	GMT + 01.00	MADRID	GMT + 01.00
ATHENS	GMT + 02.00	MELBOURNE	GMT + 10.00
BOMBAY	GMT + 05.30	MONTREAL	GMT - 05.00
CAIRO	GMT + 02.00	NEW YORK	GMT - 05.00
CALGARY	GMT - 07.00	PARIS	GMT + 01.00
CHICAGO	GMT - 06.00	ROME	GMT + 01.00
DURBAN	GMT + 02.00	S.FRANCISCO	GMT - 08.00
GIBRALTAR	GMT + 01.00	SYDNEY	GMT + 10.00
HOUSTON	GMT - 06.00	TOKYO	GMT + 09.00
LONDON	GMT 00.00	WELLINGTON	GMT + 12.00

DATE	ENTERS CANCER	GMT	LEAVES CANCER	GMT
1984	JUN 21	5.02 AM	JUL 22	3.58 PM
1985	JUN 21	10.44 AM	JUL 22	9.37 PM
1986	JUN 21	4.30 PM	JUL 23	3.25 AM
1987	JUN 21	10.11 PM	JUL 23	9.06 AM
1988	JUN 21	3.57 AM	JUL 22	2.51 PM
1989	JUN 21	9.53 AM	JUL 22	8.46 PM
1990	JUN 21	3.33 PM	JUL 23	2.22 AM
1991	JUN 21	9.19 PM	JUL 23	8.11 AM
1992	JUN 21	3.14 AM	JUL 22	2.09 PM
1993	JUN 21	8.59 AM	JUL 22	7.51 PM
1994	JUN 21	2.48 PM	JUL 23	1.41 AM
1995	JUN 21	8.34 PM	JUL 23	7.30 AM
1996	JUN 21	2.24 AM	JUL 22	1.19 PM
1997	JUN 21	8.20 AM	JUL 22	7.16 PM
1998	JUN 21	2.02 PM	JUL 23	12.55 AM
1999	JUN 21	7.49 PM	JUL 23	6.44 AM
2000	JUN 21	1.48 AM	JUL 22	12.43 PM
2001	JUN 21	7.38 AM	JUL 22	6.27 PM
2002	JUN 21	1.25 PM	JUL 23	12.15 AM
2003	JUN 21	7.11 PM	JUL 23	6.04 AM
2004	JUN 21	12.57 AM	JUL 22	11.51 AM

John Astrop is an astrologer and author, has written and illustrated over two hundred books for children, is a little Scorpio married to a little Cancerian artist, has one little Capricorn psychologist, one little Pisces songwriter, one little Virgo traveller and a little Aries rock guitarist. The cats are little Sagittarians.